Advance Praise for
Making the Choice:
When Typical School Doesn't Fit
Your Atypical Child

Can your child be gifted and at the same time have a learning disability or learning difference? The answer is a resounding yes! Learn why "twice exceptional" children often do not thrive in traditional educational settings. Explore the possibilities of tailoring an educational experience that is perfectly suited to your child through homeschooling.
— Ann Lahrson Fisher, Author
  Fundamentals of Homeschooling: Notes on Successful Family Living Homeschooling in Oregon

Finding the "right" learning environment for a child is getting more difficult each year, particularly for gifted children with advanced abilities, uneven development, and/or learning differences. Making the Choice *provides a user-friendly roadmap for parents on the challenging, and ultimately rewarding path, of helping their children reach their developmental potentials. I will be recommending this book to my clients.*
— Dan Peters, Ph.D., Licensed Psychologist
  Co-Founder/Clinical Director, Summit Center, Walnut Creek & Napa, CA
  Co-Founder/Co-Director, Camp Summit for the Gifted, Talented, and Creative, Marin Headlands, CA

With empathy and wisdom, Goodwin and Gustavson discuss a variety of considerations and offer guidance and support in finding and designing appropriate education for gifted kids. They understand that each child is unique, and that this fact requires a focus on what a young person needs in order to learn and thrive rather than on what a school might dictate. Had this book been available when my son needed something very different from what his school was serving up, I would have been more confident to begin, and begin sooner, clearing a radically different path for him.
— Wes Beach, Beach High School
  Author, *Opportunities after "High School": Thoughts, Documents, Resources*

Making the Choice is a 'frank and straight-to-the-point' guidebook for parents emphasizing their critical responsibility for ensuring a quality education for their gifted children. The authors give readers the courage to make the choice to homeschool by dispelling widely held assumptions about the disadvantages thereof and pointing out the social and intellectual advantages of teaching gifted children at home, from the early years through high school. Making the Choice *arms parents with important information to create a schooling environment where their children's minds can be stretched; where they can be exposed to a wide variety of challenging learning experiences; where they can be accelerated at an individual pace, and where they can be comfortable with being gifted—all within an honest and non-defensive setting. Highly recommended reading for any parent considering homeschooling for their gifted children!*
— Joy Lawson Davis, Ed.D.
   Author, *Bright, Black, & Talented: A Guide for Families of Gifted African American Learners*

Is school working for your child? Is he or she overcome with frustration or quietly settling for boredom? Whether your child is gifted or has gifts concealed by learning challenges, Making the Choice *helps you consider educational alternatives for your child. In a clear, readable style, it helps you examine your child's needs and your options, addressing common questions and fears. Homeschool sounds daunting, but it can save your child's education and enrich your family life. Ready to consider this from two experts who won't sugarcoat the challenges? Turn to this book as you would to a wise, experienced friend.*
—Kathy Kuhl, LearnDifferently.com
   Author, *Homeschooling Your Struggling Learner*

Making the Choice: When Typical School Doesn't Fit Your Atypical Child *is a great guide to getting started in gifted education, as well as an introduction to the reasons you might consider homeschooling your gifted child. From identification and testing to twice exceptional children, through educational options and getting to college, Goodwin and Gustavson guide readers through the potentially difficult process of understanding the gifted child and beginning to meet her social and academic needs in a safe, loving environment: homeschool. This quick guide gives just the right amount of perspective and detail when you're deciding to take the plunge and begin homeschooling your gifted child.*
— Carolyn Kottmeyer
   Hoagies' Gifted Education Page: www.hoagiesgifted.org

Making the Choice:

When Typical School Doesn't Fit Your Atypical Child

By Corin Barsily Goodwin and Mika Gustavson, MFT

Edited by Sarah J. Wilson

Dedications

To Madeline & Benjamin, who taught me all of the important things in life. I love you both so much. Wherever would I be without you? —CBG

To my parents, Sharon Lehmer Gustavson and Gus Gustavson, and my sister, Kirsten Gustavson, my first and most important teachers. My appreciation for your guidance grows yearly. —MG

Contents

Acknowledgements

We'll start with the obvious: thanks to the GHF board members and staff who have made this possible. GHF Board: Debbie Schwarzer, our legal beagle; Brandy Taylor, better known for her cheesecake; Anne Beneventi, who is always so darned positive about everything.

GHF staff & advisors: Tara Hernandez, Annette Holzman, Eleen Kamas, Wes Beach, Stephanie Hood, Madeline Goodwin. You guys are amazing in too many ways to list here.

Sarah Wilson gets our undying gratitude for cracking the whip and being world's best editor ever. There would be no completed book without you, Sarah.

We also deeply appreciate all of the GHF members, colleagues and clients whose enthusiasm propelled us when so much else took priority. A special thanks to those of you who read this book and provided feedback during the process.

Corin: Thanks to Robert Bachmann, without whose love and support my sanity would have long been a goner. Madeline & Benjamin, you have both been remarkably patient and understanding. Robert Barsily—a.k.a. Dad—the early years were tough, but you are still an inspiration to me. Camma Barsily, thanks for your many insights. Rora Thompson, I'm at a loss for words, so let's take the easy route: You rock. Gratitude also goes to Donna Ferguson, whose dog, Molly, has so helpfully provided childcare, and to Glen Margolis, Rob Heittman, and Steve Peppercorn, who are the kind of friends everyone should have.

It's somewhat unusual for one author to thank the other, but in this case, enormous amounts of gratitude go to Mika and her family (dog and cats included). Without them, the sky would have fallen a long time ago. We are family (in a good way).

Mika: Thanks first and foremost to my husband, Rich Berlin, for encouragement, understanding, fresh ideas, music, laughter, poetry, and continually bailing me out in the kitchen. A wave to the DSN (Dense Social Network), my homeschool mentors and friends of the heart who keep me grounded. And of course, a huge thank you to Seth and all the creatures, whom I love equally. You are my inspiration and my rocket fuel.

Introduction

Let's start with this: what we have to say may not apply to everyone. If your child is thriving, your family is happy, and you foresee no major changes to this situation in the future, then by all means hand this book to someone else who may benefit from it!

However, if you are like the rest of us, second guessing yourself and muddling through the parenting of a gifted, highly gifted, or perhaps twice-exceptional child, you may be seeking some advice and new ideas. One of the biggest challenges in parenting these kids is the search for an appropriate educational environment. *Making the Choice* uniquely addresses the process of determining what to do when an educational situation is not working for your child and your family, and urges parents to place the emotional and academic needs of the child at the center of the decision-making process.

Change is scary. We know that. Sticking with something that is not working is scary, too—in the long run—even if it seems easier now. It is our belief that, as parents, the final responsibility for raising and educating our children rests with us. If a situation is not working, it is up to us to recognize that there is a problem and proactively address it. After all, we adults are responsible for doing our best to provide our children with the greatest possible chance to soar.

In the chapters that follow, we will discuss how giftedness and twice exceptionality (gifted plus learning differences or "invisible disabilities") might affect the educational needs of your child. We also consider a variety of options regarding educational choices and the path to making them. We provide some questions (and hopefully answers) intended to help you make your way along this path.

The willingness to make different educational choices requires some courage. We won't promise sunshine and lollipops at the end of it, but if your current situation isn't working, you might find it's worth the risk. Many families of gifted children have taken alternative educational paths out of desperation only to discover that, once in, they wouldn't want it any other way. We hope you, too, will find what you seek.

—Corin Barsily Goodwin & Mika Gustavson, MFT

Chapter One

Assumptions and Expectations

The role of a parent is to create an environment that is safe, structured, and supportive, in which a child can explore, make decisions, make mistakes, and self-correct, in order to become an independent and self-sufficient adult.
—Mica Fuller, LMFT[1]

The quote above is a useful touchstone for many parenting and education questions. When a decision that a parent has made does not meet this standard, then the parent must reconsider the situation and possibly change the approach. If a classroom situation is not working, if the child is miserable or simply not thriving, then are you creating the environment described? Is the environment harmful or merely less than optimal? How close to optimal do you require for your child? At what point do you make changes? How do you balance the needs of everyone in the family in order to create the best environment for all, and teach your children to do so for themselves as they get older? The answers will be different for every family, but this definition makes a good yardstick.

The next question, of course, is, if the current situation is not working, what should you do? Have you failed as a parent if you let your child leave an inappropriate environment? Are you teaching them to run from their problems, or allowing them to fail? Perhaps it is possible that you are teaching them the wisdom of knowing "when to hold 'em and when to fold 'em."

Are there alternatives, and if so, what are they? For many families, private school is too costly, homeschooling is not even on their radar screen, and an appropriate charter or alternative program in their neighborhood may not exist. "Then what?" families wonder. The answer to that question is not simple or easy, with no one-size-fits all solution. What we can tell you, however, is that there are options, and some of them may be more effective for your family and your child than whatever arrangement is currently in place.

"Getting a good education" is frequently cited as a primary goal of parents for their children. But what *is* a "good education"? Is it high grades in a reputable school following a standard track en route to an Ivy League university? What if a child gets good grades in a less well-thought of program, or bad grades in a "top" school? Or that child achieves academically, but is unhappy and resentful of the direction in which she feels steered? What if a child has a learning style that does not respond well to the methods used at his school, or is intensely sensitive, or is sure that the teacher (or the other children) hates him? How much learning gets done under those conditions?

What happens when the child learns differently than how the classroom lessons or school curricula or state standards are designed? What if she has different interests, wants to learn things in a different order, or already knows what the teacher is covering just then? Is a good education strictly an academic concept, or could it extend to the whole child, her social and emotional needs as well as her intellectual needs? If your child is gifted or highly gifted, what exactly constitutes a "good education" or appropriate education for your child? Does it necessarily equate to the same education that other children are getting, or is it possible that every child has different educational needs, including the need and the right to be challenged to learn new ideas and meet his own individual potential?

Parents generally assume that the year their children turn five years old, they will send them off to kindergarten. The children will use scissors and paste, learn the alphabet, and maybe even learn to read. They'll sit quietly while the teacher reads stories to them, and use manipulatives to familiarize themselves with basic mathematical concepts such as number recognition and counting. It will be fun, and parents will proudly display their children's artwork on the refrigerator at home. When the parents go in for their first parent-teacher conference, they will meet the wonderful lady (it's usually a lady, isn't it?), maybe for the first time, whom they have entrusted with their children's introduction to the world outside of their home, and they will be told how sweet their children are and how well they have learned to play with others. They will have no worries.

It's a nice fantasy, isn't it?

In fact, that's all it is—a fantasy—for the millions of families with children who, for one reason or another, do not fit in well at school. The reasons are endless: they have big personalities; their teachers have expectations that the children can't or won't meet; the children's development isn't suited for that particular environment; the children learn in a different style or at a different pace than the other students do or the teacher is prepared to accommodate; and on and on. At some point, parents face a moment or a series of moments, where they have to wonder if the school or classroom their child attends five days out of seven is the right environment for their child.

Some parents face this defining moment early, when their six-year-old, who has completed the Harry Potter series, has a meltdown each morning when it's time to get ready for school, or when their eight-year-old requests a physics textbook for her birthday, despite her marginal grade in science. For others, their child may appear to fit into the school environment fairly comfortably before it dawns on the parents that something is askew with this picture, that the fantasy and the reality simply are not mapping well. And then they ask, what happened? Is it them? Is it the child? Has the school failed them? And they wonder, "What am I going to do now?"

Some parents don't even reach that point. They see their child struggling academically, emotionally, or socially in a school environment and they do everything they can think of to help. They discipline the child to motivate him to do his homework. They provide tutoring in reading, math, and social skills. They change classrooms or teachers. The child may have an individual education program (IEP), which is a legal document that outlines agreed-upon accommodations that the school district is bound to implement. Maybe the child is accelerated or given harder homework, and perhaps those parents still have a nagging feeling that something is not right.

Most of these options involve changes to the child or slight changes in the environment, but they all have something in common: each one assumes that the child should fit into the classroom through effort or force, and that any problems stem from that direction. They all assume that the traditional classroom is the right place for the child. But what if we stopped holding the environment relatively constant while changing the child, and instead let the child be who she is while changing the environment?

Most adults in the United States today grew up attending school in a traditional classroom, and their default assumption is that their child will do the same. The parents who did not enjoy school assume that if they survived it, so can their child. The parents who loved school would not want to deprive their child of what they imagine to be the same wonderful experience. Others may simply defer to those whom they see as educational "experts" without really considering options. It's true that seeking alternatives requires a great deal of effort on the part of the parents. It can be a paradigm shift, a lifestyle change. We are then forced to reexamine our values, our priorities, our hopes and expectations for our children. That's no small project! More and more families are coming to this point, however, with the onslaught of standards-based curriculum and limited resources for gifted children in the school system. As we gain better understanding of what it means to be gifted, we also realize how poorly we as a society have met the needs of these children and how much more we must do.

Chapter Two
Your Atypical Child

The term "gifted" is sometimes used to describe well-behaved, high-achieving students. No doubt these children are truly gifts to the harried teacher or administrator, but it is a mistake to apply that term only to children who fit a description of "well-behaved" and "high achieving." We know that some gifted children misbehave, acting out their boredom and frustrations. Some are not academic achievers. Some have emotional challenges. Some have learning differences or learning disabilities along with their giftedness. This is hardly a uniform lot!

Attempts to understand giftedness have resulted in a wide variety of descriptions, each focused on a particular component. The brain researcher will take note of an individual's neurological asynchronies, while the therapist may see a high level of sensitivity as a primary issue. The education professional working through a school district commonly uses as a guideline an intelligence test score above 130 (depending on the test), which is two standard deviations above the average IQ score of 100. Some programs that are ostensibly for gifted children search for the top 2-5% of the population as shown by various determinants, while others look for significantly advanced scholastic achievement (based on chronological expectations).

One description of giftedness is based on the child's differences from the norm in ways that encompass more than intellectual ability alone:

> *Giftedness is asynchronous development in which advanced cognitive abilities and heightened intensity combine to create inner experiences and awareness that are qualitatively different from the norm. This asynchrony increases with higher intellectual capacity.* **The uniqueness of the gifted renders them particularly vulnerable and requires modifications in parenting, teaching and counseling in order for them to develop optimally.**
> —The Columbus Group, 1991 (emphasis added)

This takes into account the unique characteristics of the child and specifically highlights the necessity of charting an educational and parenting course that meets the needs of the individual child as they are. This is no easy thing, and naturally any parent would want more information before embarking on a different and less-traveled path.

Unfortunately, we live in a society in which the term *different*, especially when applied to children, is equated with "needs to be fixed." Parents and teachers, in need of reassurance or simplification, evolve practices based on the theory that children develop at more or less the same rate and in the same way, based on books they have read or child development theories with which they are familiar. When a child does not respond as expected, the assumption is that something about the child needs to be corrected. It is a rare occurrence when others notice and understand that a particular child's behavior is, in fact, quite normal—that is, normal for a gifted or 2e child—and that a gifted child does not always excel at everything, all the time. Instead of being identified as gifted and then appropriately educated, they may end up falling through the proverbial cracks.

Gifted Identification

Many experts have found that parents, when *given sufficient information about giftedness*, are actually the best identifiers of it in their children. Dr. Linda Silverman, director of the Gifted Development Center in Denver, Colorado, specializes in assessing children for giftedness. She writes that 84% of the children whose parents bring them to her for testing say that the children fit three-quarters of the most common gifted characteristics (see list on page 10) and the children also score at least 120 IQ (in the superior range) on standard tests of intelligence (IQ tests). A score of 130 IQ or higher usually indicates giftedness, but giftedness is not a yes-or-no concept and test scores are not the sole indicator of a gifted child. Silverman further finds that, while over 95% of the children brought to her show giftedness in at least one area or subtest, some may be asynchronous in their development and have areas of weakness that can depress their apparent full scale IQ scores to a number below the accepted threshold for giftedness. For this reason, it is important that anyone doing quantitative IQ testing for giftedness have some knowledge of and experience with this population, as well as a strong understanding of how to interpret the resulting scores.

The list of gifted characteristics on the next page is a handy tool for preliminary identification of giftedness. While not all gifted children display all of these behavioral traits, if your child has a preponderance of them, it could be an important clue.

Parents and teachers may also find it helpful to think of this list as a range of normal traits and behaviors for gifted children, and therefore a tool to assist in distinguishing between potentially pathological behaviors in a non-gifted child and typical characteristics of the gifted. Because gifted children are often more intense than non-gifted children, this could be an issue in many situations. For example, a gifted child who is emotionally intense may cry easily and often, but this does not necessarily equate with emotional immaturity. A child who has trouble sitting still and learning at the same time may not have

ADHD, but instead could be a kinesthetic learner who needs to move her body in order to efficiently operate her brain. The child whose nose is stuck in a book may not be ignoring you when you call him; he may simply be hyperfocused on the world of his imagination and did not register that you were addressing him (hint: try gently touching him to get his attention).

Some Possible Characteristics of Gifted[2]

- Reasons well *(good thinker)*
- Learns rapidly
- Has extensive vocabulary
- Has an excellent memory
- Has a long attention span *(if interested)*
- Sensitive *(feelings hurt easily)*
- Shows compassion
- Perfectionist
- Intense
- Morally sensitive
- Has strong curiosity
- Perseverant in their interests
- Has high degree of energy
- Prefers older companions or adults
- Has a wide range of interests
- Has a great sense of humor
- Early or avid reader *(if too young to read, loves being read to)*
- Concerned with justice, fairness
- Judgment mature for age *(at times)*
- Is a keen observer
- Has a vivid imagination
- Is highly creative
- Tends to question authority
- Has facility with numbers
- Good at jigsaw puzzles

Testing 1, 2, 3

For many children, a formal assessment of their ability and potential is unnecessary. If they are succeeding in their environment, and seem to be learning well and emotionally healthy, then a formal assessment might just be a diversion of resources away from other activities or instruction from which the child might benefit. However, there are several types of assessments and many reasons why having one could be in the child's best interest as well as providing useful data for parents in determining the child's needs.

When you have more questions than answers, you should consider having your child assessed. For example, you might want to have an assessment done when your child is perfectly capable of telling a great story, but refuses to write it down under pain of death, or takes three hours to do what appears to be a fifteen-minute assignment. Maybe your child gets even more frustrated than you do at the state of her room, yet seems unable to organize her belongings in order to clean it. Perhaps your child returns home from a long day of classes or activities far more exhausted than you think he should be. When your child's behavior impacts his or her learning, self-esteem, relationships or ability to participate in otherwise enjoyable activities, it may be time to seek an outside evaluation.

Parents who plan to homeschool often assume an assessment is unnecessary, since they aren't trying to qualify for school services or programs. In fact, parents who are seeking useful insight into the way their child thinks and learns may well see the value in such an investment. An IQ test administered properly, by a professional who is specifically familiar with gifted and 2e characteristics and issues, can provide a wealth of information to which you can refer when making choices about parenting and educating your child.

Another reason that some families who homeschool choose to have their children assessed is that their children may wish to attend gifted and talented camps, programs and institutions which require test scores as part of their application process. However, if this is your primary reason for testing, it is recommended that you first check with the programs that interest you to see which test results they accept.

The most common evaluation option is a quantitative assessment, in which your child will be asked to answer a variety of questions using more traditional tools such as the ones used in the WISC IV (Weschler Intelligence Scale for Children, Fourth Edition). These tests, which are subdivided into such areas as general knowledge, block or pattern design, and working memory, can provide insight into possible underlying neurological issues and may also be helpful in uncovering learning difficulties, such as auditory or visual processing disabilities, which are not otherwise apparent. Most gifted children will have relative strengths and weaknesses—in other words, they are not *globally gifted*—and the picture created by a good assessment of your child's brain can be an incredibly helpful tool for both parenting and educating them. Some gifted children have significant hidden weaknesses or disabilities, and they truly suffer because they don't understand why they struggle to write or spell or do math computation or get organized. They feel stupid and are frequently treated as such, despite their many overshadowed strengths. A formal assessment can help identify such weaknesses. For more information on testing, see http://www.hoagiesgifted.org/testing.htm or http://giftedhomeschoolers.org/articles.html#testing.

An evaluation can also be qualitative in nature, where a certified professional spends time with your child in addition to reviewing background information that you have provided. Based on the test or measurement tool used, the testing professional can give you an estimated range of full scale IQ, as well as assist in pinpointing specific learning differences or other neurological challenges faced by the child. As with a quantitative assessment, they will refer you to a specialist to address those challenges. Many of those specialists can also be the first stop in the evaluation process, whereby a child with, for example, a known auditory problem, can go directly to an audiologist, or a child with sensory issues can be evaluated by an occupational therapist at less time and expense. It all comes back to what questions you are trying to answer.

When seeking professional help, finding a good match *for your child* is critical. Specifically, search for a tester who actually has experience working with a variety of gifted children. If you hear the phrase "Oh, I test profoundly gifted children all the time," consider the speaker's reputation. Unless this is a nationally-known expert who attracts clients from all over the country—or at least a well-known local practitioner serving an area with a high concentration of gifted adults—the claim is a statistical impossibility. It probably indicates a lack of knowledge and comprehension on the part of the supposed expert, and we suggest you run screaming. (O.K., screaming is optional.)

You should look for a tester who understands how gifted children process input and can interpret the subtest scores that make up the test results. He or she should be able to translate the results into meaningful information that you, as a parent or other adult in the child's life, can use. Most importantly, try to find someone who can think creatively. It's rare that gifted kids fit neatly into predetermined categories, and you will benefit from working with someone who can make the necessary leaps in thought.

We do recommend you keep in mind that the resulting numbers dancing across the test page should be interpreted based on a comprehensive picture of the child in question. There should be a clear understanding that they provide a neurodevelopmental snapshot rather than a permanent profile of your child's brain or intelligence quotient (I.Q.). It's also important to note that children may have similar full-scale test scores, but the scores may mean something different in each child. For example, the various tests are weighted more or less heavily in certain areas and are thus not directly comparable. Also, because subtest scores are based on a child's performance in the various portions of an assessment, a significant spread between any of them is generally considered an indicator of learning differences or at least areas for further inquiry.

Even when all subtest scores are above average or higher, a child may experience frustration or other difficulties resulting from a significant *relative* weakness. When a child is able to zoom ahead in most areas but has limited hand-eye coordination for handwriting, for example, or insufficient working memory for a project they are assigned, the combination of frustration and feelings of inadequacy can be highly potent. Keep in mind that seemingly "analytical" skills like math involve tremendous amounts of imaginative, dreamy, associational thinking; and seemingly "abstract and creative" skills like painting or sculpting involve tremendous amounts of detailed planning.

A subtest score in the gifted range does not, then, preclude a designation of twice-exceptional (2e), a term that is used to describe a person who simultaneously displays giftedness and other learning challenges.

Levels of Giftedness

One of the major misunderstandings about the term "giftedness" is that it is believed to be a one-size-fits-all category. The truth is that the range of human abilities can be broad and diverse throughout any given segment of the population. The generally accepted rule is that the average IQ score is 100, and one standard deviation (SD) is approximately 15-16 points. Most school systems use two SDs, or 130 IQ, as the minimum score required to qualify for gifted programs. Yet, this leaves no room for margins of error at the cutoff. It also assumes that a single "gifted and talented" program is all that is needed to meet the diverse needs of a group of gifted and twice-exceptional children.

Think about it this way: It is already acknowledged that a child with an IQ score that is 30 points above the norm would be better served in a specially designed program for gifted students. If you then have a child whose IQ is yet another 30 points higher, is it not reasonable to assume that this second child needs an even further differentiated educational program? Additionally, the higher up the IQ scale you go, the more likely you are to encounter diversity among the learning abilities and styles of these children. Remember, we previously said that a single IQ score can mean different things in different children? That's because the higher FSIQ (Full Scale IQ) scores are usually representative of a wider range of subtest scores, increasing the likelihood of twice-exceptionalities, as well.

The chart below, borrowed from Carolyn Kottmeyer in *What is Highly Gifted? Exceptionally Gifted? Profoundly Gifted? And What Does It Mean?* [3], breaks down the range of giftedness into more informative subsets. (As always, these are guidelines, not to be clung to in a hide-bound and slavish manner.)

Level of Giftedness	Full Scale IQ score WISC-IV, WPPSI-III source: Assessment of Children	Extended IQ score WISC-IV source: Technical Report #7 WISC–IV Extended Norms and publisher's 2008 NAGC presentation	Full Scale IQ score SB-5 source: Ruf Estimates of Levels of Giftedness	Full Scale IQ score WISC-III, WPPSI-R, SB-4, SB L-M
gifted or moderately gifted (G or MG)	130-138	130-145	120-129	130 – 145 (132-148 SB-4)
highly gifted (HG)	138-145	145-160	125-135	145 – 160 (148-164 SB-4)
exceptionally gifted (EG)	145-152	160+	130-140	160 – 180 (SB L-M only)
profoundly gifted (PG)	152-160	175+	135-141+	180 and above (SB L-M only)

Twice Exceptional (2e) and Asynchronies

> *...because of their enhanced sensitivity, gifted children tend to learn with fewer repetitions, and to need less extensive explanations in class, although it is important to remember that their sensitivity may be modality specific (that is, hearing, seeing, kinesthetic) rather than across the board. Enhanced sensitivity also frequently results in enhanced distractibility, and gifted children may at times be suspected because of this to have ADHD. However, it is important to remember that in gifted children, distractibility is frequently accompanied by considerable persistence, and even though their attention seems often to wander, so long as it keeps returning to the task at hand and the work gets done, it should not be considered an impediment. In fact, there is considerable evidence that such "distractibility" is one of the roots of creativity. Enhanced sensitivity that results in impaired learning, however, whether because of distractibility to visual, auditory, tactile, or other sensory cues, is a real problem that requires evaluation and treatment.*
>
> —Drs. Brock & Fernette Eide[4]

As noted previously, most gifted children have some asynchronies, or uneven areas, where they are more or less advanced than in other areas such as motor planning, decoding, auditory memory, eye-hand coordination, sequencing, or spatial awareness. Areas of weakness are not unusual in *any* child because children do not develop at a predetermined pace and in lockstep. In a gifted child, however, you may find that the uneven or asynchronous rate of development manifests in a variety of ways, not all of which are academic. Your darling little seven-year-old may have insights worthy of an adult, the attitude and eyeball rolling attributes of a teenager, and the hissy fits of a preschooler! This is a challenge for the adults doing their best to communicate with these unusual young people, but it makes sense when you think about it from the perspective of the 2e child. Consider having the knowledge to imagine a much more complex art project than you are physically capable of producing due to difficulties with eye-hand coordination, or being unable to follow directions due to auditory processing disorder—and as a result getting stuck with work of a much lower level of difficulty because no one, including yourself, realizes that you are capable of so much more. Gifted children often have an emotional adherence to truth and justice and a passion for same, but that does not mean that their perception of what is fair is the same as yours, because in life experience they are still only children.

These well-intentioned children may not only be out of their depth in experiences, they may also have difficulties in sequencing ideas or sorting through logic or summarizing or drawing appropriate conclusions. Or, they may have an expressive language disorder that prevents them from articulating their concerns in a constructive fashion. These children end up appearing stubborn, pushy, and possibly not very bright, as opposed to the gifted-but-challenged young people they truly are. Furthermore, exposure to concepts that are beyond their emotional development while they are fully capable of understanding the implications (such as war, homelessness, or even an adult argument) could result in emotional distress that children with some neurological disorders may be unable to process effectively, or which may cause stress that leads to an increase in manifestation of symptoms.

While these behaviors are all within the range of "normal" for a gifted child, some gifted children experience more extreme asynchrony, where the gap between their greatest areas of strength and their points of weakness are significant enough to fall into the category of serious learning problems or disabilities. These kids are still considered gifted, but because they have relative or functional learning or attention difficulties, they are what we call "twice exceptional," or "2e." They are gifted and *also* have a learning disability or deficit.

A child who is considered 2e can easily be misdiagnosed, because giftedness and learning differences often have overlapping symptoms. Frequently included among these conditions are ADD/ADHD, autistic spectrum disorders, auditory and visual processing disorders, or other emotional or mental disorders. Often, professionals misdiagnose children who are twice exceptional because they are unfamiliar with the various disorders, as well as with the concept of common co-morbidities and the myriad presentations of twice exceptionality. They may not know which questions to pose to parents, and the parents may not know which behaviors to describe to the professionals.

Because many of these conditions manifest similarly, it is critical to understand the root cause of these behaviors, whether it is due to a neurological condition or the child's exhaustion in the face of continually pushing against her limitations. These children are often able to compensate for any weaknesses extraordinarily well for a period of time, and so long as they are performing academically at the assumed level of or ahead of their age peers, the possibility of a dual (or multiple) designation just is not considered. In some cases, the learning difficulties may mask the giftedness, while in other cases the giftedness masks the weaker, problem areas. This is why it's not always easy to spot a child who is twice exceptional, particularly if he doesn't want to be spotted.

Frequently, twice exceptional children are identified when parents seek assistance in understanding seemingly incomprehensible behaviors on the part of their child. For example, there could be neurological dysfunctions causing a child to take two hours to complete a 20-minute math assignment when the child clearly understands the material. There could also be emotional outbursts such as refusal to attend a favorite activity when a substitute teacher is leading the class.

A similar marker of possible twice exceptionality in a gifted child is the level of frustration the child faces. Many parents and teachers don't understand why a child has a hard time with something that the adults don't believe should be difficult. Despite behavioral clues from the child, they still don't suggest assessment, in the hope that if the child would only try harder he will figure it out and be able to do it on his own. That's a lot like expecting a paralyzed child to get her physical fitness in the same manner that all of the other children get theirs, in spite of the limitation on the individual child's ability to perform in that manner. We have seen children whose learning disabilities are not discovered until their teen or even young adult years. These children could have been spared a lot of frustration, pain, and destruction of their self-esteem if the disability had been discovered and addressed or remediated sooner. In fact, many parents do not learn to identify and understand the implications of their own learning challenges until they start doing the research on their children, recognizing the similarities between the way their child presents symptoms and the way that they did as children—and often still do. One thing many 2e kids do for their parents is to offer a mirror to look into that may be helpful, or may cause resentment to those who prefer not to know.

Learning differences (LDs) are often called "invisible disabilities" because they are not obvious at first glance, leading adults to assume that the child is being lazy or stubborn. While some LDs can be overcome through sheer effort, the adults involved need to consider whether this is something the child can truly work through, or whether some kind of academic accommodation or professional assistance would be helpful. Is it fair or reasonable to ask a child to expend additional effort overcoming obstacles when there are minimally intrusive mitigating therapies that can be undertaken, many of which may be covered by standard medical insurance or even the local school district? And from the point of view of the child's education, is it fair to keep a child struggling with an area he is not developmentally ready for at the expense of surging ahead in his area or areas of strength?

Being twice-exceptional poses major challenges for both the child and the significant adults in their lives. Failing to identify, or incompletely identifying, the special needs of these children makes the possibility of constructing an appropriate learning environment a much higher hurdle. Happily, with identification and intervention, a satisfying and successful educational experience is within reach.

> *Children with learning disabilities, behavior disorders, or other types of school problems who are also gifted in one or more areas must be allowed to be gifted in their areas of strength while they receive assistance in their areas of need. The discrepancy between their superior abilities and their dramatic weaknesses results in feelings of inadequacy, frustration and hopelessness. Many of these students are at high risk of becoming school dropouts. To bring sanctions against any child which prevents them from experiencing differentiation whenever or wherever it's needed is simply not effective or fair.*
> —Susan Winebrenner[5]

Chapter Three

When the Classroom isn't Working

Gifted Programs

Some school districts acknowledge the different academic needs of gifted students by offering one of a variety of programs within the regular school setting. Magnet schools, for example, allow potential students to apply for admission into a stand-alone program where students identified as gifted are taught separately from their neurotypical age peers. Some districts embrace differentiation within the individual classroom, where gifted students are given work to do that is of greater breadth or depth. Still other districts have pull-out programs where the gifted child is excused from their regular classroom to participate in advanced academic or enrichment classes. Of course, all of this assumes that gifted programming is a priority for the district, and that resources are available for this purpose.

There are diverging opinions regarding what constitutes a successful gifted education program. There are a lot of factors to be considered, including available resources, how a gifted program is weighted against the many other programs a school might wish to fund, and the lack of specific knowledge and understanding of gifted educational needs by those who make the final determination regarding how district money is spent. In the event that there *is* a gifted program available for your child, there are no guarantees that that particular program is going to be a good fit.

If your child is twice exceptional, gifted education programs are even less likely to fully accommodate his needs. Most gifted education programs tend to be rather limited in scope (if they exist at all), as if there were only one type of giftedness and one type of program that would fit the needs of all. There is no single solution to the education of gifted children, largely because there is no prototypical gifted child. As a result, while most program administrators work hard to meet the standards put in place for them, those standards are not necessarily appropriate for the particular children being served. This sets everyone up for failure. A preferable approach would be to cede ownership of success to the individual child when possible, with assistance from parents and professionals.

Sometimes when a parent hears others raving about how wonderful or how "good" the local gifted education program is, they wonder why it doesn't seem quite so fabulous to them. If their child does not happen to fit the model for whom that program was designed, however, it does not mean that the child is not gifted nor does it mean that the child or the adults have failed in some way. It simply means that the program in question is not the right one for that child and the search for the right program must continue.

Bow Tie Model

For those of you who prefer a visual image of why 2e kids may not get their needs met in the traditional classroom, consider the diagram on the next page.

We start with a number line with 100 at the center and a standard deviation (SD) of approximately 15. The circle in the middle has a diameter of 1-2 standard deviations (SDs). In that circle, you have most children in the typical classroom (represented by the light dots). Their intellectual potential and their learning styles are close enough to the other 20-30 children that a single teacher with a predetermined curriculum can likely give them the education their local school district intends.

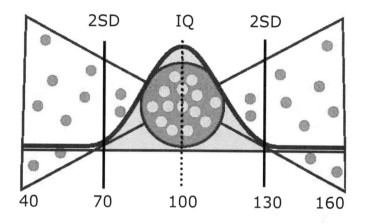

Now consider the remainder of the line on either side of the circle. The pair of triangles on the number line, each centered on the line and each pointing at opposite sides of the circle, is reminiscent of a bow tie. The children who fall either into the triangle at the higher end of or into both triangles on the scale (represented by the darker dots) are the gifted and 2e children who do not fall into the circle of relative educational comfort. Some of those children may be capable of successfully participating in the classroom given sufficient differentiation or accommodation, but none of them have the same needs as the children in the center. At least as much to the point, they don't all have the same needs as each other.

Nobody would reasonably expect a child with an IQ two or more SDs below the norm (approximately IQ 70) to thrive in a mainstream classroom, nor should they expect it from a child with that much difference above the norm. Remember, a child with a measured IQ of 160, for example, is as far from the child with an IQ of 130 (often the cutoff for acceptance into school-based gifted programs) as the child with an IQ of 130 is from the child of IQ 100.

To further complicate matters, twice exceptional children—especially those with abilities measurable at both ends of the bow tie—

have asynchronies, learning styles, and academic potential that are significantly different from the "pleasantly gifted" child (IQ ~125-145). The pleasantly gifted child has the competitive advantage of high intelligence without the disadvantage of being too different. The individual learning styles of 2e children, however, are virtually guaranteed to be such that they will need significant deviations from the educational norm.

As a result, despite efforts to steer all students towards a quantifiable level of academic attainment each year, this goal is not often achieved for 2e children in spite of their high levels of intelligence. The ideal situation for these children would be a program allowing them to learn at their pace and in their own manner. Unfortunately, few traditional classroom situations have the resources to accommodate these children to their fullest extent even when their needs are recognized.

Whose Fault is It?

Parents whose children have not received "the free and appropriate public education" to which they are legally entitled will understandably advocate ever more forcefully. They will try to talk to the teacher or the school principal, perhaps seeking to initiate an IEP. They may request assistance from medical or mental health professionals or attorneys. Some parents have been very successful at negotiating accommodations for their gifted or twice exceptional child, and are able to continue working with their school district to obtain an acceptable education for their child. Unfortunately, this is not always the case. The amount of time and effort involved may be more than many parents are able to spare, or the participants on the school's professional team may simply be unwilling. Sometimes the problem is a lack of human or financial resources. At some point, you have to ask yourself whether you are getting a reasonable return on your investment. It may be that the energy involved in advocacy is better spent on pursuing an alternative educational approach. Your primary concern is not fighting for help that isn't available; it's supporting your child and determining the next step on the path.

A very common concern for parents who are considering pulling their child out of a toxic educational environment is the fear that they are teaching their child to run away from adversity. However, as adults, when we find ourselves in a situation that does not fit us well, we usually have some control over our choices. We can stay and attempt to make reasonable accommodation, we can request assistance, or we can leave. As adults, we consider this a matter of good judgment. Children are often stuck in situations that cause them discomfort (or worse), with no choice and no escape. This can be especially damaging if they are not sufficiently articulate or confident in their ability to be heard in order to improve their situations. It's very important to listen to the child and to play detective, rather than simply taking to heart comments and advice from other adults. Other people's impressions can be useful, but if they are not trained in identifying gifted and 2e issues, or have other concerns that color their perceptions, their input may not be on target. Your best course is to do your own homework: gather data from multiple sources, consider what you know about your own child and what resources are available to you, and work from there.

Many families wonder how they will know for sure that it is time to try an alternative method of educating their child. The right educational arrangement for your family is the one that gets the most needs met for the most people at the time. The answer is different for every child and every family, and is likely to change with circumstances and experience.

Red Flags and Other Concerns

As parents, educators, and other adults concerned with doing the best you can for the gifted children in your lives, you would like to think that you could see when a school situation isn't working, and that you could fix or change it. Yet, it doesn't always work that way.

Sometimes you won't recognize the cause of the problem, or perhaps you will fail to recognize its seriousness. You may be unfamiliar with the issues at hand, or under pressure from relatives, friends, and neighbors to take (or not take) specific actions without sufficient consideration of the needs of your children or yourself. You may not even be aware of any actions you could take. Sometimes as a mere mortal you will succumb to human error, denial, or false hopes. Still, you need to do your best for your children, even when that means reaching beyond your own comfort level to try something different.

Let's say you do have an inkling that something is not right, and you think the problem might be a mismatched environment. What are some of the signs you might notice? What does "school is not working" look like?

Examples of possible red flags

- resistance in going to school or doing homework
- refusal to participate in activities
- poor grades
- unwilling to turn in assignments because they "aren't perfect yet"
- taking way too long to complete seemingly simple projects
- anger, irritability, agitation
- self-loathing or negative self-talk
- anxiety or excessive worry
- withdrawal
- significant alteration in their social lives

Sometimes, though, a child is getting good grades and appears to be doing "just fine," yet the parent has a sense that something may be wrong. Keep in mind that getting good grades is only an indication that the child is accomplishing the tasks her teacher has told her to accomplish, in the manner in which they have been laid out to be accomplished. Just as poor grades don't necessarily indicate a lack of intelligence, good grades don't necessarily indicate a good fit nor an appropriately challenged student.

For example, if a child has the ability to go further with an idea than what is needed to get an "A," yet is loaded down with busywork and told that an "A" is the pinnacle of success, what incentive does he have to go beyond? When feeding a hungry brain on insufficient rations, the brain (i.e. the child) will get along O.K., but it won't thrive. Moreover, a child may become clinically depressed, develop problem behaviors, or possibly abandon the pursuit of education entirely by dropping out or giving up. The point is that while poor grades may be a red flag, good grades are no guarantee that all is well.

Interpersonal challenges associated with the educational environment will also negatively impact a child's ability to learn. These warning signs can be more difficult to decipher because the cause-and-effect sequence isn't always clear. This type of situation may require you to delve more deeply into your child's feelings. You and your child may also benefit from the assistance of a therapist or other knowledgeable professional to sort through the tangle of emotional complexities.

Less obvious red flags

- Lack of connection or positive relationships with teachers and fellow students. For example, a gifted child is likely to be highly sensitive to how adults perceive her—a gifted child who is convinced her teacher doesn't like her is probably not fully engaged in classroom activities. Similarly, a child who worries about bullies or who is exceptionally lonely is not a child whose brain is focused on learning.
- Physical illness due to stress. Some gifted children manifest very real symptoms such as stomachaches and headaches, sleep disturbances, or other physiological complaints.
- Missing out on important family time. A child may spend an unreasonable amount of time struggling with inappropriate

homework rather than interacting with his family, or he may resent the adults who pressure him to conform to expectations that he is not well equipped to meet.

Ignoring the Red Flags

Sometimes problems are easy to spot, but other times they are not. What you see as a parent may not tell the full story about whatever is happening to your child. Gifted children are masters at camouflaging their feelings and keeping the meaning behind their behaviors to themselves, if they even understand it themselves. It's not always apparent that a minor change in attitude is not developmentally appropriate, but instead may be indicative of a serious problem. As parents, we need to trust our instincts. After all, if you address a problem that turns out to be minor, that's still a good thing, right?

There are all sorts of potential negative consequences for a child left to struggle in an educational environment which is a poor fit.[6] Social isolation or simply feeling "different" can be a big problem for these children. This can come about through academic boredom, repeated experiences of seeking shared interests with peers and failing, or through the well-intended implementation of whatever pull-out program a school may have for its gifted pupils. Once a child feels "other," she is also at significantly increased risk for depression, suicidal thoughts, and other actions of self-harm. Depending on the educational environment and its responsiveness, a gifted child may also be the object of teasing, bullying and ostracism because of his "otherness," leading to more isolation, depression, or anxiety.

Other consequences of unaddressed academic boredom can manifest as a child who withdraws into her own world or who loses the academic curiosity that so fired her up when she first began learning about the world. Many kids lose their joy of learning in the process of being educated, but for gifted children the consequences can be startling and especially distressing. One child we know began kindergarten already reading at a third- to fourth-grade level. He was bubbly and eager to soak up every new thing his mother showed him. But a combination of being held to the pace of his more typical classmates and his developing sense of wanting not to "stick out" caused him to lose ground every year. By the time he reached sixth grade, he was just short of failing his classes, acting out at school, and worrying his parents about what other behaviors he might engage in just to pass muster with his peers. Indeed, as kids get older and the pressure to conform becomes greater in the school, the efforts to which many gifted children go to "pass" can increasingly damage their academic development and emotional well-being.

An even more pernicious consequence of academic boredom lies in the place where perfectionist tendencies meet up with low expectations. A child who never experiences success in the face of adversity can fail to learn tenacity and will avoid challenges if she can, especially if her tendency is to fear not being perfect in the first place. Further, if the child gets high marks without working hard to earn them, is this an indication that she is performing well, or that we don't really know what her potential is because she not sufficiently challenged? This is one of those times where perfectionism, a typical characteristic of gifted individuals, combines with aspects of a poor fit in the classroom to create a perfect storm of a problem. That problem sometimes spins out further, with a child actively avoiding or refusing work so that his internal belief in his own "stupidity" is not found out.

Sometimes the negative consequences hinge on a gifted child's intensities and sensitivities, and their interaction with an environment, rather than on interpersonal experiences. These are some of the most mystifying happenings for parents. One young mother could not understand why her toddler, who loved singing and making music together at home, cried and clung to her at her local "kiddie gym" where she went for mommy and me classes. It was not until years later when she recognized her daughter's sensitivity to sounds and sights that she understood that the hard-edged, bright primary colors of the gym, combined with the live acoustic space and lots of children running around, was overstimulating for her little girl and resulted in her melting down. In another instance, a father we know was enthusiastically encouraged by his professional colleagues to bring his two children to a local amusement park. They had all been there, and characterized the place as "family friendly." He had to work hard to explain to his colleagues that this attraction might be a lot of fun for their kids, but the visual and auditory chaos that the amusement park would represent to his twice exceptional, profoundly gifted children would be anything but friendly for his family.

School environments can be just as prone to environmental pitfalls as kiddie gyms or amusement parks, and have the added difficulty of being an all-day, every-day proposition for most school children. It is often a surprise to discover that the reason that child in the back isn't paying attention isn't due to boredom or disinterest in the topic, but because the fluorescent light is emitting a high pitched noise that almost no one else can hear yet is driving him to distraction. Or perhaps the reason the bright young girl isn't doing her homework is because she has trouble with visual focus and by the time she looks up at the assignment on the blackboard and then down to her desk to write it down (and back again, several times), the class is over and the teacher has erased the information in preparation for the next class taught in that room. The child is unable to get the full assignment noted accurately, and so will not be able to turn it in on the following day.

The fallout from problems that are not addressed doesn't only affect the children themselves, but their entire families. Just as a child is not an isolated individual, so the challenges created by giftedness are not experienced by the child alone, but by the parents and siblings, and even the extended family. There are family "ripples" that come out as stress between parents, discord between siblings, and family problems for the gifted child that exacerbate any educational situation. Family dynamics can take a hit in many ways. It can be easy for one child to become characterized as the "good" child and another as the "bad" child, based on how much effort has to go in to dealing with them. This in turn can lead to self-esteem and self-image problems for both the "good" and "bad" children, which can also be played out in the sibling relationship. For example, a 12-year-old girl we know lorded it over her younger sister that the sister's behavior at school was creating stress for mom, and that the 12-year-old was mom's favorite because of it.

Another pitfall is when one sibling feels neglected because of all the attention given to another sibling, arising from the problems of the school's poor fit for the gifted child. There are meetings and conferences and evaluations and appointments, all of which eat away at time for the sibling, as well as free time and resources for the family as a whole. As the problem of how to fix the gifted child so that he fits in gets addressed, the tendency is to focus on what is wrong. Parents and other adults get so caught up in what a child's weaknesses are that the child does not get an opportunity to enjoy his strengths.

The family distress over the problems created by poor academic fit can also bleed into multi-generational issues, where well-meaning grandparents and other relatives weigh-in on, and take sides over, the problems their children and grandchildren are facing. Imagine being a mom who is trying to meet the needs of a hurting child, a school that demands conformity, a sibling who wants more time, an employer who wants to see work deadlines achieved and meetings attended, a spouse who just wants the whole situation to be resolved peacefully, and her own mother, who is full of advice about how her child can be a better parent. It's overwhelming, and it's no surprise that some parents feel they just can't handle it.

Now, we aren't saying that being in school will cause all the problems above to materialize, nor are we saying that homeschooling will make them all go away. We are saying that failing to pay heed to signs of trouble, telling yourself that your child will grow out of them, or minimizing their import is likely to result in things getting more difficult, not less. It may be challenging to dive in and sort through the problems, but the alternative is worse. One way or another, you're going to have to do the work.

Chapter Four

Educational Alternatives

The Process

When an educational setting isn't working as it should, the usual first step is to seek out accommodations or modifications that meet the child's needs within the existing environment. Perhaps a child is not progressing as expected academically or is disrupting the other students. In the public school, the child then gets referred for further observation and possibly an IEP, although the level of implementation and comprehensiveness of this program may vary. In private schools, the situation will likely be handled differently, as they are not legally required to fully accommodate your child. In any case, there are processes that you can initiate and resources to mobilize.

Ideally, a written and signed agreement between you and the school would address your child's needs sufficiently that she could fit into the environment and succeed based on goals as decided upon by the adults involved. Unfortunately, this is often more theory than practice. Regardless of what you do or do not have on paper, accommodations won't necessarily change attitudes, expectations, or beliefs, and a skeptical or uncooperative teacher or intolerant classmates can create an unhealthy environment for a gifted child. The simple fact of having accommodations may make the child's "differentness" more visible to others. Additionally, accommodations imply that unique needs are somehow a problem to be fixed rather than characteristics that make up a valuable individual human being. Sometimes suggested accommodations are not about altering the environment so much as about altering the child so they can fit into the environment. That might not be best for your child, day in and day out, until high school graduation.

Things to consider

- When things are not working out, how far are you willing to go to accommodate for your child's needs? What are the trade-offs?
- How comfortable is your child with assistance both academically and socially?
- Is your child using more than his or her allotted share of the school's or household's (often limited) resources?
- Does a teacher resent you as a pushy parent or your child as a classroom management problem? This can impact communication, as well as the learning environment.
- Are the other kids teasing yours? Your child needs to know that he deserves decent treatment rather than simply enduring abuse for lack of an alternative.
- Is your child complaining about the accommodations intended to help her?

None of this is meant to imply that your child does not have the right to a free and appropriate public education, nor even that the answers should automatically lead you to radically alter your choices. However, any time you make a change you should be aware of the consequences, whether they are academic, financial, or emotional.

Each child should be considered carefully—who he is, what his unique needs are, and what gets him interested. Picture a situation where your child was happy, excited, and eager to learn. This might not necessarily be in the context of his current educational situation, but at summer camp or working with a mentor or exploring on his own. What would best allow your child to thrive—if money and time were no concern? With whom does he best relate? What does he enjoy doing? How does he learn most effectively? What does he want to learn?

Consider also what the greatest obstacles to your child's learning might be. Is her current educational situation a good match for her learning style? Does she interact well with those around her, or, given a choice, would she prefer something different? Does she enjoy learning a bit at a time or in big chunks? When is your child happiest?

If your child is old enough, engaging him in this process can be highly beneficial. (Even a child of six or seven can be involved in decisions about his education to some extent.) When you begin to tailor a learning experience to the specific individual needs of your child, he is validated as a thinking and feeling human being. Many gifted children have strong opinions about school (and many other things) from an early age. They like to be respected and validated for their broad interests, their advanced thinking abilities, and their opinions. We have found that they welcome the chance to have input into their education, and we believe such involvement will help them learn to advocate for themselves as the school years go on into their teen and college years, and into adulthood.

Choosing from a menu of educational possibilities, a child can set the pace of her learning and work from a variety of materials. She has the opportunity to pursue interests and take advantage of strengths while leaving room to address weaknesses without loss of dignity. This reinforces a child's self-confidence as an intelligent individual, rather than negatively emphasizing how she may be different from other students.

Oftentimes we may hear others say that children should simply learn to adjust to what they are given, or that a child will benefit from grounding in the same institutional setting that "all the other children" are experiencing. Yet, our public education system groups children by chronological age and assumes they learn in the same way and at a similar pace. Typically, seven-year-olds are in second grade. In reality, we must keep in mind that all seven-year-old children are different and their experiences in any given setting may be different, as well. Sometimes, in spite of our best efforts as parents and teachers, a particular setting may not actually be a situation in which a child will perform well. For example, a seven-year-old gifted child may already be reading books aimed at the sixth-grade level or higher. She may be reading the Harry Potter series. She may be creating complicated puppet shows or doing multiplication and division problems. The mismatch of a typical second grade classroom for a child like this may simply be too great. Although it is nobody's fault, a mismatch exists and must be addressed.

The Options

Many families of gifted children have walked away from full-time traditional classrooms over the past several years, having discovered the academic, social, and emotional benefits to allowing their children time for a more individualized educational approach. Once upon a time, homeschooling was considered the domain of people who wanted to raise their children outside the influence of mainstream culture; however, changing educational policies have driven a more diverse population to seek alternatives to public schools.

There are many alternatives to a traditional classroom environment, and the possibilities are growing in number all the time. As the number of families seeking options grows, so do the number of services available to them, and the more services, the easier it is to weave together an educational experience that suits your child. Further, as many educational professionals recognize the need for alternatives, the more they are willing to work with parents to find creative solutions. Sometimes these solutions are formal programs, and sometimes they are more homegrown, but ultimately, they all serve the purpose of helping the next generation find their way.

Once upon a time, the common image of homeschooling involved a mom and her kids sitting at the kitchen table immersed in workbooks. There are still many families who choose to recreate a school-like learning environment at home, but there are many more who have added to or replaced this method with group activities, online courses, field trips, project-based learning, and taking classes at educational centers or community colleges. Some states offer homeschoolers the opportunity to attend classes on a part-time basis, plus many districts offer independent study programs (ISP), as well as charter schools and private programs.

Many families that are new to alternative education are most comfortable enrolling their child in a distance learning program, in a charter school, or through an ISP. These options generally involve working within certain guidelines as determined by the program administrator, and may include pre-specified curriculum in addition to monthly or quarterly meetings with a teaching supervisor. These options provide some familiar structure and support, and can be a good stepping stone between full-time school and other alternatives, as those become clearer. A potential benefit to these choices is that someone other than the parent is guiding the child's education; the child is accountable to an outsider, thereby minimizing what could be a major focus of power struggles in some families. These programs often allow either full- or part-time enrollment, and the brick-and-mortar programs often have campus classes or field trips in which the children can participate. One caveat, however, is that you'll want to discuss any learning or procedural concerns (such as grade placement, testing, or acceleration) with program administrators in advance, lest you find your child in a program with the very rigidity you were seeking to escape.

A more independent school-at-home approach involves purchasing curriculum by subject or as a package and spending a given portion of the day essentially mimicking a school day, less the recesses, waiting in line, and waiting at a desk bored or daydreaming while the other students catch up. Families who do school-at-home generally find that they can get through an entire day's worth of material in just a few hours, leaving the rest of the day for children to play sports, take recreational classes, or follow other interests. Something to keep in mind with the school-at-home model is that gifted kids don't necessarily learn at a steady pace. Sometimes they need time to assimilate new information, while other times they rocket through a year's worth of material in a week. Any curriculum or materials purchases should be made with that in mind.

Not every family will choose to use a pre-formatted course of learning. Many homeschoolers do "unschooling" or "eclectic homeschooling," both which generally translates to child-led education. The parent's job is to help the child identify interests and follow up on ideas by offering them appropriate activities, materials, tutors, or mentors as needed, and otherwise gently guiding and encouraging them. No rule says that any child must study using a particular style of learning, so these inherently flexible options often become the methods of choice for families of gifted children. Once a gifted child has "recovered" from any emotional disequilibrium brought about by a poor fit in his previous educational experiences, he is likely to look around and find things that interest him. Gifted children tend to be self-motivated, when given the opportunity and assistance with any obstacles (such as learning differences), causing many parents of gifted children to be accused of pushing their children to achieve when in fact those parents are simply running to keep up with them. Should you choose to homeschool, your child may prefer a lot of time at home for mental processing of what they are learning, or you may find yourself running around wondering if you should purchase a cute little chauffeur's cap.

Many parents who consider homeschooling their children without formal structure and support worry about who will teach the subjects that they are not well versed in. Some families find tutors and mentors in adult professionals, while others enroll their academically advanced students in community college in addition to or instead of other homeschooling choices. This has become much more common in recent years. The U.S. Department of Education reported several years ago that 98 percent of community colleges and 77 percent of public four-year colleges were taking part in dual-enrollment programs.[7]

Regardless of the approach they take, families pursuing non-traditional educational choices often spend a lot of time out and about in their communities, using life activities as learning tools. They might participate in various classes, visit the library, do service projects, meet with mentors who are more available during the typical school day, visit a museum or other field trip site, or even travel around the country or the world! Families can take advantage of these many opportunities to enhance the joy of learning while meeting a child's individual needs.

Transitioning from the Schoolhouse

So what can a parent expect of this transition? Each family, and each child within that family, is unique and each factor should be weighed based on the family's personal values rather than defaulting to that of the local community. Some parents make the choice to try something alternative, yet quickly find that the solution they had placed their hopes in to solve the problems facing their child is not proceeding the way they expected. The decision to leave the traditional school setting is usually based on a search for a more harmonious, less stressful experience. Often parents expect that leaving school will result in immediate peace and tranquility at home. Over the long run this often is the case, but the short-term may be more of a challenge.

One thing that contributes to this challenge is the process that children go through when changing settings, regardless of the reason for the change—from one school to another, from school to not school, or some other combination. The process of moving from one paradigm of learning to another can be confusing, and the psychological messages instilled in an inappropriate setting don't vanish right away. In fact, for children who have been emotionally damaged by their schooling experiences, things often get worse before they get better. A parent who decides to homeschool is likely "taking the bull by the horns" and solving problems that the school district can't or won't. But the change in the child isn't immediate.

Our advice to you at this stage is: Don't be too quick to evaluate your new situation. It may take several weeks or even months on both the child's and parent's part to get used to new expectations, new routines, and new aspects in the relationships between family members. For children, this adjustment largely revolves around what the shape of the day is now and what the new expectations are for them. For a child who has experienced failure in living up to expectations before, it's reasonable for them to be anxious, stubborn, or even defiant until they have enough experience with the new model of their day to feel comfortable. The issues of trusting their parent become even more thorny if previously the parent had joined in with the school in exhorting the child to change their behavior. There may have been damage done to the parent-child relationship at that point. Allow time to repair that damage.

The major challenge for parents is learning what their role is, how much or little structure works for their child, and unhooking from previous expectations. Trusting their child's process is very anxiety-provoking for many parents. They wonder how long to allow their child to stay focused on one interest or how long before their child's interest is piqued. They worry about grade-level progress. This is all normal. It is a parent's job to worry about their child. Just hang on and let the process unfold, trusting your child's natural drive to learn and grow. Listen and provide guidance, but don't feel you need to do the learning for him.

Given the temperament of many gifted children, with tendencies toward overexcitabilities and emotional intensity, it is probably wise to expect a "roller coaster" experience. The good times will be intoxicating, and the bad times will be sobering indeed. Picture a

2e child, finally able to devote herself to the depth of study in a preferred area that she craves. Sunshine! Picture that same child, running up against surprises in her routine, or being asked to try to do something she associates with her weaknesses, or her unpleasant experiences at school. Storms gather, and sometimes burst. Or perhaps you have a "rainbow" weather child: sometimes clear and beautiful, sometimes cloudy. Our best advice to you at this point is to hold on and let the storms clear. Make decisions about what is or is not working once there is some adjustment to the new arrangements.

Can a parent smooth the process? Yes, emphatically. The most beneficial thing is to plan for stormy weather, and if your child is old enough, help him expect it as well. Then when the time comes, it is much easier to identify the challenges and not to get too worried about them. The unprepared parent will worry if this is the new standard they can expect from their child; the savvy parent will understand it is just a stage in the transition.

As this transition, positive though it may be, is inherently stressful for everyone in the family (the parent taking on the new task of educating the child, the child experiencing the transition, and perhaps a child or children who are remaining in the traditional setting), it can be helpful to get support for the process. You are very likely to run into those folks who are adamantly against homeschooling in any form, and who are not shy about letting you know overtly or otherwise. You may also discover that many parents feel inherently judged by you when you make a choice that is different from the ones they make for their family, and those people—sometimes friends— whom you had no intention of judging will get defensive or put distance between you. There are no easy answers for how to deal with this except to take it as it comes and remember that *you* are the one who is raising your children—your friends and in-laws are not. One thing that can certainly help with this struggle is finding other local families who have left the schoolhouse and learning what their transition was like. Search out, or create, a support group for parents of gifted children facing similar issues. Many are already available online, or you can look into starting your own.

Another useful mindset is to go into this process without over-planning. The more flexible you are in your thoughts about what your new educational arrangements will look like, the more likely you are to be able to tweak them to suit your particular needs. Understandably, guiding your child's education may seem like a huge leap in responsibility when you have, until that point, relied on the school district and other "experts" to guide the education of your child. It is not surprising that you may feel somewhat disconcerted or overwhelmed, or even unqualified, when urged to assert educational independence. In truth, there are as many ways to educate a child as there are children and families: many do not require a great stretch of the imagination, while others require extensive stretching!

Chapter Five

Considerations

Academic Outcomes (and Getting into College)

If the child is homeschooling into the high school years, some families worry about whether they can provide academic excellence in a nontraditional setting. In fact, data show that—across racial and socio-economic lines—homeschooled children reach levels of academic achievement similar to or higher than their publicly schooled peers.[8]

Parents and grandparents also wonder if alternative educational situations might impact college admissions. They need not worry. Students are increasingly able to enroll in college without a traditional high school experience. Many colleges and universities have actively sought homeschooled children for years, while others have recently joined in the chase. These institutions include Ivy League settings, state universities, small liberal arts colleges, and programs with a strong focus on science and technology.

Homeschooled students have shown themselves to be well-prepared, too. Research shows that a greater proportion of homeschooled students go on to college than their traditionally schooled counterparts. Additionally, homeschooled adults attained higher educational levels compared to the general U.S. population in the same age range.[9]

What about Socialization?

Go to your local public school, walk down the hallways and see
what behaviors you would want your child to emulate.
—Manfred B. Zysk

A great deal of mythology has sprung up based on homeschool families who isolate their children from others, resulting in partially educated, socially dysfunctional teens or adults. The truth? Research shows that homeschooled students as a group exhibit more appropriate social behavior than their traditionally schooled counterparts.

One study of college students that had been homeschooled found that they "had significantly fewer problem behaviors than their public school counterparts."[10] Another study showed that—across every measure—formerly homeschooled adults were more likely to participate in civic activities such as voting and community involvement than same-aged adults in the general population.[11] Statistics further show that homeschooled adults are more likely than the general population to consider themselves very happy, find life exciting, be very satisfied with their work, be satisfied with their financial situation, and believe that hard work is the most important determinant of success.[12, 13]

Gifted children are sometimes stereotyped as asocial geeks who think like computers and can't ride a bike or throw a football. Some opponents claim that this is proof of the need for them to be in a "normal setting." After all, these people claim, those children need to learn to get with the program, like all the other kids. However, as Louise Porter writes in *Social Skills of Gifted Children*,[14]

. . . most of their social problems arise when they do not fit with
the surrounding children: gifted children lack true peers rather
than lacking peer relationship skills. This means, then, that one
of the main ways to foster these children's relationships with other

youngsters is for them to have access at least occasionally to like-minded peers.

The common wisdom in our society is that children need chronological peers in order to make friends and be happy. This is not necessarily the case. Gifted children in particular need developmental and intellectual peers, and the same asynchronies that sometimes separate them from their age peers in the classroom also come into play in forming satisfactory friendships. According to longtime gifted researcher Miraca Gross, "children's conceptions of friendship . . . form a developmental hierarchy of age-related stages, with expectations of friendship, and beliefs about friendship, becoming more sophisticated and complex with age." In *"Play Partner or Sure Shelter": What gifted children look for in friendship,* Gross lists five levels of conceptual complexity, and just as with any other neurophysical stages, the more highly gifted the child, the more likely she is to be advanced beyond her age peers, and thus remain unfulfilled in her relationships with them.[15] The happiness of true friendship may not lie in the other eight-year-olds on the playground, but in the elderly gentleman who teaches piano and incidentally shares his love of music and his own history with your child, or with the girl three years older who doesn't care much about boys and makeup but is really keen on sharing her Tamora Pierce books and learning about reptiles.

Given the freedom to pursue their own interests, many homeschooled gifted children will find enjoyment, challenges, and friends of similar interests through signing up for art classes, Lego® robotics, knitting circles, or athletic programs. Others will also (or instead) take private lessons in activities or topics of their choice. In addition to finding other kids who share their interests or abilities, these situations can provide both intellectual challenge and role modeling from an adult other than the child's parents. The opportunity for a gifted child to work with an adult—be it a private sewing instructor or a graduate student at a local university who shares the child's passion for string theory—can turn into a mentoring relationship or even a strong friendship that will hold the child in good stead for years to come. After all, most every child needs adults in their lives beyond just their own parents, if only to experience the diversity of humanity and the basic lessons in socialization, Besides, many gifted children can relate better with adults, because the adults often treat them more respectfully and are more tolerant of a younger person's individual quirks than many children will be. It can be difficult to find appropriate mentors for these bright children with sometimes obscure or uncommon childhood interests, yet it is crucially important to do so in order to provide them with role models of what a successful gifted adult might look like.

Parent-Child Dynamics

Many parents seem reluctant to spend long stretches of time with their children. This may be due to the intensities brought about by overexcitabilities in either the parents or the children. It may also be that, frankly, some children find themselves in situations so untenable that they lose abilities they may have acquired to control their pain, anger, and frustration, and they take it out on the people closest to them. Some children are so frustrated due to lack of understanding (by themselves or by you, their teachers, etc.) that they just seem permanently miserable. Still others may simply be dealing with hormones or another perfectly normal (though unpleasant) stage of development.

We can't tell you that homeschooling will solve every relationship issue you might have with your children, but we can state definitively that many families find it helps tremendously to spend more time with their children and to make more effort to get to know them— something you can't help but do if you are homeschooling. You can adjust the amount of time you spend rousting them from bed, rushing them around, and battling over homework. Just by removing the pressure and accepting them as the unique individuals they are, you are likely to see light at the end of the tunnel—and not the headlights of an oncoming train, either.

Chapter Six

Making the Choice

Educating gifted children has special challenges, with solutions as unique for each family as the children involved. Gifted children are not always easily identifiable within the school system and their needs range far beyond any one-size-fits-all solution. There are myriad options for educating these children, at least some of which may be feasible for the ones in your care.

As a parent, you don't have to settle for "good enough" and you don't have to jam your square peg into a round hole. You have the opportunity to construct a flexible, fluid solution that allows your child to flourish.

As a society, we must realize that our current system of education does not provide sufficiently for the diverse needs of these gifted children who represent our future. While we should continue to advocate for systemic change, transformation is unlikely to come quickly enough to meet the needs of the children who are struggling *now*. The negative impact of a single traumatic school year may seem negligible to those of us who have lived for decades, but in the life of a child, it feels like forever. Being asked to tolerate an inappropriate or even harmful environment for so long can take a great emotional and academic toll.

Our children deserve the best we can give them. You've heard the saying, "I brought you into this world and I can take you out"? We're not advocating taking your child out of life, as Bill Cosby humorously suggested, but taking them out of school might be just the ticket. You have choices.

Once again, we'll remind you that what works for one child won't necessarily work for another. You, as the parent, know your child and your family best, and have to make the best decisions you can with the data you have available. Go ahead and use your judgment even if it means leaving the familiar behind. It may be uncomfortable and the road will be bumpy, but a trip off the beaten track can lead you to all sorts of wonderful experiences you might otherwise have missed.

Appendix: Now What Do I Do?

So you've read the book, made your choice, and now you want to know what to do. Here are some of our favorite resources for finding information about giftedness and about homeschooling.

Gifted Resources

Websites

Gifted Homeschoolers Forum
    http://giftedhomeschoolers.org/
Hoagies' Gifted Education Page
    http://hoagiesgifted.org/
SENG (Supporting Emotional Needs of the Gifted)
    http://sengifted.org/

Books

Bright, Talented, & Black: A Guide for Families of African American Gifted Learners, by Joy Lawson Davis

Raising a Gifted Child: A Parenting Success Handbook, by Carol Fertig

Misdiagnosis And Dual Diagnoses Of Gifted Children And Adults: ADHD, Bipolar, OCD, Asperger's, Depression, And Other Disorders, by James T. Webb, Edward R. Amend, Nadia E. Webb and Jean Goerss

Homeschool Resources

Websites

Gifted Homeschoolers Forum
    http://giftedhomeschoolers.org/
Homefires: The Journal of Homeschooling Online
    http://www.homefires.com/
A to Z Home's Cool
    http://homeschooling.gomilpitas.com/

Books

Creative Homeschooling: A Resource Guide for Smart Families, by Lisa Rivero

The Teenage Liberation Handbook: How to Quit School and Get a Real Life and Education, by Grace Llewellyn

Fundamentals of Home-Schooling: Notes on Successful Family Living, by Ann Lahrson-Fisher

Endnotes

[1]Mica Fuller, "Conflict Accountability Program Curriculum." San Jose, CA (2006).

[2] Dr. Linda K. Silverman, *Characteristics of Giftedness*, http://www.gifteddevelopment.com/What_is_Gifted/characgt.htm (2011).

[3] Caroline Kottmeyer, *What is Highly Gifted? Exceptionally Gifted? Profoundly? And What Does It Mean?*, http://www.hoagiesgifted.org/highly_profoundly.htm (March 29, 2010).

[4] Drs. Brock and Fernette Eide, *Brains on Fire: The Multimodality of Gifted Thinkers*, http://www.neurolearning.com/Brains%20on%20Fire_%20The%20Multim odality%20of%20Gifted%20Thinkers.pdf (December 2004).

[5]Susan Winebrenner, *The Hollingworth Center for Highly Gifted Children*, (Fall 1998 XII).

[6] Kipling D. Williams, *Professor: Pain of ostracism can be deep, long-lasting*, http://medicalxpress.com/news/2011-05-professor-pain-ostracism-deep-long-lasting.html (May 10, 2011).

[7] June Kronholz, *High Schoolers in College: Dual enrollment programs offer something for everyone*, http://educationnext.org/high-schoolers-in-college/ (Summer 2011).

[8] Tanya K. Dumas, Sean Gates, and Deborah Schwarzer, *Evidence for Homeschooling: Constitutional Analysis in Light of Social Science Research*, http://ssrn.com/abstract=1317439 (December 17, 2008).

[9] *Ibid.*

[10] Brian D. Ray, "Home Schooling: The Ameliorator of Negative Influences on Learning?," *Peabody Journal of Education* 75 (2000).

[11] Richard G. Medlin, "Predictors of Academic Achievement in Home Educated Children: Aptitude, Self-Concept, and Pedagogical Practices," *Home School Researcher* 10 (1994).

[12] Joe P. Sutton and Rhonda S. Galloway, "College Success of Students from Three High School Settings," *Journal of Research & Development in Education* (Spring 2000).

[13] Patrick Basham, John Merrifield, and Claudia R. Hepburn, *Home Schooling: From the Extreme to the Mainstream, 2nd Edition*, http://www.fraseramerica.org/researchandpublications/publications/5411.aspx (October 4, 2007).

[14] Louise Porter, Social Skills of Gifted Children, http://www.agateny.com/Article_SocialSkills.html (2010).

[15] Miraca U. M. Gross, "'Play Partner' or 'Sure Shelter': What gifted children look for in friendship," The SENG Newsletter (May 2002).

About the Authors

Corin Barsily Goodwin founded GHF in 2004 to address a growing need for support and advocacy. Prior to that, she served as the Gifted/Special Needs Advisor for the HomeSchool Association of California and co-chaired their Legislative Committee. She has been presenting workshops on giftedness, learning differences, and homeschool related issues for many years. Her articles have been seen in *NAGC (US) Parenting for High Potential, 2e Newsletter, California Association for the Gifted's Gifted Ed Communicator*, the *NAGC UK Magazine, California HomeSchooler, SENG Update, Thinking Person's Guide to Autism*, and many other publications. Ms. Goodwin also serves on the SENG Editorial Board and the Advisory Board of the Asynchronous Scholars' Fund. She lives in the woods of Southern Oregon where she homeschools her 2e children with the help of two cats and a turtle who live with her, and a dog who just thinks she does.

Mika Gustavson, MA, MFT is a counselor who specializes in helping the gifted to thrive. A homeschooling mom herself, she specializes in providing support to families considering paths-less-taken in learning, nurturing, and parenting. She leads groups and classes for parents of gifted, quirky, intense, anxious, and twice-exceptional children, as well as providing trainings and presentations for educators and other professionals on issues touching on giftedness, homeschooling, and parenting. Ms. Gustavson serves on the Gifted Homeschoolers Forum's Professional Outreach Committee, and is a community board member for Camp Summit for the Gifted. She works and lives in Silicon Valley, with her husband, son, and an ever-changing menagerie.

Made in the USA
Lexington, KY
25 July 2011